HOT DESERTS

Rose Pipes

RSVP
RAINTREE
STECK-VAUGHN
PUBLISHERS
The Steck-Vaughn Company

Austin, Texas

Published by Raintree Steck-Vaughn Publishers,
an imprint of Steck-Vaughn Company

A ZOË BOOK

Editors: Kath Davies, Pam Wells
Design & Production: Sterling Associates
Map: Sterling Associates

Library of Congress Cataloging-in-Publication Data

Pipes, Rose.
  Hot deserts / Rose Pipes.
    p. cm. — (World Habitats)
  "A Zoë Book"—T.p. verso.
  Includes index.
  Summary: Introduces some notable deserts around the world,
including the Sahara Desert in Africa, the Sonoran Desert in North America, and the Simpson Desert in Australia.
  ISBN 0-8172-5004-2
  1. Deserts—Juvenile literature. [1. Deserts.] I. Title.
II. Series: Pipes, Rose. World habitats.
GB611.P55 1998
577.54—dc21
                                          97-9071
                                             CIP
                                           AC

Printed in Italy
Bound in the United States
1 2 3 4 5 6 7 8 9 01 00 99 98 97

Photographic acknowledgments

The publishers wish to acknowledge, with thanks, the following photographic sources:

Robert Harding Picture Library 16; The Hutchison Library / Angela Silvertop - title page; / Wilkinson 5; Impact Photos / Alan Keohane 9, 18, 20; / John Evans 12; / Bruce Stephens 21; NHPA / Anthony Bannister 8; / Dan Griggs 15; / Lady Philippa Scott 19; ANT/Bill Bachman 25; South American Pictures / Tony Morrison 26, 29 / Robert Francis 28; Still Pictures / T de Salis - cover background; / Klein/Hubert - cover inset bl; / M & C Denis-Huot 4; / J.P.Delobelle 7; / John Newby 11; / Werner Gartung 13; / Christian Testu 27; TRIP / Eric Smith 23; Woodfall Wild Images / Adrian Dorst 17; / Ted Mead 22; Zefa - cover inset tr, 10, 14, 24.

The publishers have made every effort to trace the copyright holders, but if they have inadvertently overlooked any, they will be pleased to make the necessary arrangement at the first opportunity.

Contents

All the words that appear in **bold** are explained in the Glossary on page 30.

What Are Hot Deserts?

Deserts are very dry places. Rain may not fall there for many months or even years. Deserts may be sandy or stony, flat or covered with mountains.

In this picture of a desert in Algeria, you can see rocks and sand. The big waves, or ripples, in the sand are called **sand dunes**.

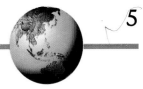

In the daytime, a hot desert may be 104°F (40°C) in the shade. But even the hottest deserts can be cold at night. In winter, frost lies on the ground in the early morning.

Deserts are windy places. Strong winds blow up thick dust or **sandstorms** that can last for days. Usually people try to protect their eyes, mouth, and nose from the blowing sand.

People hurry home as a sandstorm begins in Africa.

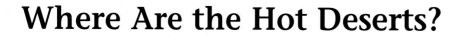

Where Are the Hot Deserts?

The biggest desert in the world is the Sahara in Africa. It is almost as big as the entire United States. Some parts of the Sahara are stony and mountainous. Other parts are sandy and flat.

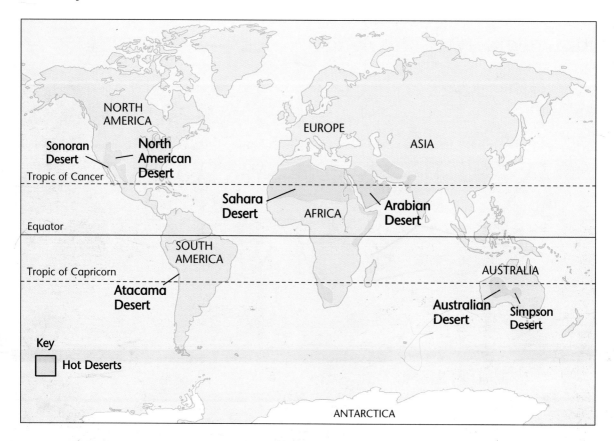

This map shows the world's hot deserts. The hottest deserts are close to the **Tropics**.

Wind and water make some of the shapes we see in deserts. Heavy rain carries away sand, stones, and rocks and makes deep gashes in the ground. Rivers, too, cut into the desert rocks to make deep **canyons**.

Strong winds blow sand and stones against the rocks to carve out very strange shapes. Together, wind, sand, and water cause **erosion** that wears away the rocks.

These rocks are in Utah.

Desert Plants and Animals

In desert **habitats** many animals burrow underground to keep cool. Each animal has its own way to escape the heat.

The camel stores food in its hump and can live for days without water. Its large feet stop it from sinking into soft sand. Its long eyelashes keep sand out of its eyes.

Some plants store water in their stems or leaves. Others grow long roots to reach underground water. These plants have **adapted** to desert life. It has taken many thousands of years for this to take place.

There is water in the desert at an **oasis**, either in pools or under the ground. People come here with their animals for water, food, and to buy and sell goods. Farmers can grow crops here. There are small towns around some oases.

This oasis is in southern Morocco, Africa.

The Sahara Desert in Africa

The Sahara Desert crosses twelve countries in North Africa, including the Sudan and Libya.

In the sandy areas of the Sahara Desert, the wind blows the sand into small ripples and tall dunes. The shape and size of the dunes may change.

No plants grow in some parts of the Sahara. There, animals hunt other creatures for food. Many animals hunt at night when it is coolest.

A small African fox, the fennec, lives in burrows. Its large feet stop it from sinking into sand, and its fur keeps it warm on cold nights. Another Sahara Desert animal that burrows is the jerboa.

The fennec has large ears that help it to stay cool and to hear sounds a mile away.

There are salt mines in the Sahara Desert. The Tuareg people of the Sahara have been salt **traders** for hundreds of years.

Now the Tuareg guide tourists through the

The Tuareg carry the blocks of salt across the desert on camels. The salt shown here came from Mali.

desert. They also make money by renting camels to them.

When oil was found in the Sahara, desert life changed. People moved in to drill oil wells. There are new roads and airports because of the oil trade. Tourists can use them to get to the desert.

Oil workers move around the desert in cars and trucks. Here they are checking an oil well in Tunisia.

The Sonoran Desert in North America

The Sonoran is the biggest desert in North America. It is famous for its cactus plants.

The saguaro cactus grows up to 49 feet (15 m) high and can live for 200 years. Cacti take in water through their roots.

The cacti and other plants that grow there are well adapted to the heat, cold, and dryness. Cacti store water in their thick, fleshy stems.

Many desert animals need cacti to live. The pronghorn, also called the American antelope, eats prickly pears. Birds and insects also eat cactus fruits.

This Gila woodpecker nests in a saguaro cactus. When the woodpecker leaves, other birds will move in.

The Sonoran Desert is cold in winter and very hot in summer. It is also dry and dusty. Highways through the desert link towns and cities, such as Phoenix and Tucson.

The largest city in the Sonoran Desert is Phoenix. It is the capital of Arizona. In this picture you can see the city, with the desert in the background.

Water for farmland comes from the Colorado River, which is 336 miles (541 km) away. The river water is carried in pipelines, trenches, and tunnels to the farms.

Phoenix gets its water from under ground and from rivers. Other cities have water pumped from places where it is stored.

A farmer rides a mule in the Sonoran Desert.

The Arabian Desert

The Arabian Desert lies between the Red Sea and the Persian Gulf. Part of it is called the Empty Quarter, an area of 251,000 square miles (650,000 sq km).

The Empty Quarter is almost as big as Texas. It is mostly sand dunes, like those in this picture. In summer it is too hot for people to live there.

The sand gazelle lives in the Arabian Desert. It eats the leaves of desert plants for food and water.

Many gazelles died because sheep and goats ate their food. Others died because people hunted them for their skins and their long horns.

Today there are **wildlife preserves** in the desert. There gazelles and other creatures have food to eat and are safe from the hunters.

A sand gazelle searches for food.

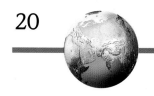

The Bedouins were once **nomads**, who moved their sheep and goats around the desert to find food and water. They rode camels to get from place to place.

Now, most Bedouins live and work in towns near the coast. Some still keep animals in the desert. Most of them use trucks, not camels, to travel around.

There is oil under the desert and the Persian Gulf. This oil has made the Arabian Desert countries, like Saudi Arabia, very rich.

Many desert towns and cities have fine new buildings and shopping malls. Many of the streets are lined with trees. They also have beautiful parks with flowers, trees, and lakes. It costs a lot of money to provide water for the plants, lakes, and fountains.

The city of Abu Dhabi is on the Persian Gulf.

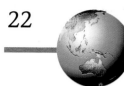

The Simpson Desert in Australia

Desert covers nearly half the **continent** of Australia. The driest part is near the center and is called the Simpson Desert. Rain may not fall in this desert for years. It is an empty place, with no towns or farms.

This is Chambers Rock in the Simpson Desert.

Part of this desert is stony. When rain falls there, flowers grow. They soon die, leaving seeds that only grow into plants when it rains again.

The Simpson Desert is famous for its long, straight sand dunes. Some of these are as long as 135 miles (220 km).

This picture of the dunes was taken from an airplane.

More than 230 kinds of lizards live in Australia. The thorny devil, or moloch, lives in the desert. It eats up to 5,000 insects a day!

The thorny devil has adapted to dry places. Its folded skin traps tiny drops of water that run down the folds into the lizard's mouth. This may be all it drinks for months, or even years.

At the southern end of the Simpson Desert is Lake Eyre. This lake is the largest one in Australia. In most years, there is no water in the lake, only glittering white salt.

If it rains hard, Lake Eyre fills with water. Thousands of birds, including the pelicans, fly to the lake when it is full. These birds, named Australian pelicans, take food and water from the lake.

Pelicans at Lake Eyre.

The Atacama Desert in South America

The Atacama is the driest desert in the world. In some parts of the Atacama, rain has not fallen for more than a hundred years. Winds blow across the desert from the ocean

The desert lies between the Andes Mountains and the Pacific Ocean in northern Chile, South America. There are cliffs where the desert reaches the ocean.

carrying sand far inland. Some animals and plants live deep in the desert, but most of them live near the coast.

Fog forms at the coast and rolls inland across the desert. The water droplets in the fog are the only water that some desert animals have to drink.

Chinchillas were hunted for their fur and nearly died out. Now, farmers raise these animals on **ranches**.

The chinchilla eats roots, grasses, and insects in the desert. It has soft gray fur.

People lived in the Atacama thousands of years ago. They found a **mineral** called copper in the rocks. They drew this metal from the rocks and made jewelry and ornaments with it.

This strip mine for copper in the Atacama Desert is the largest in the world.

Today, copper is mined and sold to other countries. Some small towns grew up around the mines in the desert, but most people live near the coast.

Antofagasta, in Chile, is the largest city on the coast. Ships carry the copper from here to countries all over the world.

The moisture from the fogs that roll in from the ocean is collected and stored. It is used to provide fresh water for the city.

Part of the port at Antofagasta.

Glossary

adapted: If a plant or an animal can find everything it needs to live in a place, we say that it has adapted to that place. The animals can find food and shelter, and the plants have enough food in the soil and enough water. Some animals have changed their shape or their color over a long time, so that they can catch food or hide easily. Some plants in dry areas can store water in their stems or roots.

canyon: A deep opening in the ground. There is often a river or stream at the bottom of a canyon.

continent: One of the seven large landmasses in the world. They are Europe, Asia, North America, South America, Australia, Antarctica, and Africa.

erosion: The wearing down of earth or rocks by the action of water, wind, or ice.

habitat: The natural home of a plant or animal. Examples of habitats are wetlands, forests, and grasslands.

mineral: Something that is usually found in rocks. Metals such as gold, silver, and copper are all minerals. They are often dug out of, or mined, from the ground.

nomads: People who move around all the time rather than living in one place.

oasis: A place in a desert where there is water. The water may be in pools on the ground or just below the ground. Plants such as date palms grow in oases.

ranches: Large farms where cattle, sheep, or other animals are raised.

sand dunes: Mounds or small hills of sand made by the wind. They are found in deserts and next to oceans.

sandstorms: When the wind blows very hard over a sandy place, the sand is lifted off the ground and blown around. This is a sandstorm. It is hard to see and to breathe in a sandstorm.

traders: People who buy and sell, or exchange, goods.

Tropics: The part of the world where the weather is hot most of the year. These areas lie between the tropic of Capricorn and the tropic of Cancer. Lines on world maps and globes show where the Tropics are.

wildlife preserves: Areas of land set aside for wildlife to live in.

Index